NEW ORLEANS
COOKING

Designed by Sally Strugnell
Recipe photography by Peter Barry
Recipes styled by Bridgeen Deery and Wendy Devenish
Introduction and captions by Ros Cocks
Edited by Jillian Stewart

CLB 2989
© 1993 Colour Library Books Ltd, Godalming, Surrey, England.
All rights reserved.
This 1993 edition published by Crescent Books,
Distributed by Outlet Book Company Inc., a Random House Company,
40 Engelhard Avenue, Avenel, New Jersey 07001.
Printed and bound in Singapore
ISBN 0 517 07298 X
8 7 6 5 4 3 2 1

NEW ORLEANS
COOKING

CRESCENT BOOKS
NEW YORK · AVENEL, NEW JERSEY

INTRODUCTION

New Orleans has an adventurous and colorful history that is reflected in its lively cuisine. As a city it has proved to be a survivor, its overriding French and Spanish character remaining largely intact even now long after the city's union with the American States. To appreciate the basis of New Orleans cooking with its Creole and Cajun specialties, it helps to know how this famous southern city came into being.

A steaming, malaria-infested swamp on the northside of a large crescent on the Mississippi was an unlikely spot for settlement, but it was here in 1718 that the French adventurer Jean Baptiste Le Moyne decided to put down anchor having pushed forth upriver from the Gulf of Mexico. There was hard work to be done raising the land from the swamp and convicts were brought out from France to do the labor. It was claimed fortunes were to be made, and French settlers came out and built themselves a city.

French settlers did not come from France alone. In the mid 1700s the British expelled the Canadian French from Acadia (now Nova Scotia) and these outcasts made their way down the St. Lawrence River, across the plains and then down the Mississippi until they reached the bayou country around the settlement of New Orleans. Here French was spoken, and they could put down roots without persecution. They made their homes largely in the bayou country to the south and west of the city. The southern American drawl transformed the name of these new settlers from 'Acadians' to 'Cajuns.' In 1762 the city came under Spanish control, but as has been proved, the French and Spanish can live harmoniously and this development did not cause great upheaval. Rather, a whole new culture came into being. They intermarried happily and the Creoles were born, the definition of Creole being: one of French and Spanish origin born in the New World.

Thus is New Orleans made up of adventurous peoples, who have acquired a suitably robust and equally adventurous cuisine. They took the indigenous ingredients, for the most part river- and seafood, and the Creoles added chili peppers and tomatoes from Spanish Mexico. They tamed the swamps and grew rice to make jambalayas like the Spanish paellas. The Cajuns borrowed the sassafras leaf from the local Indians to thicken their stews and make gumbo. Now, the two cuisines overlap considerably. Louisiana has become one of the country's greatest rice producers, and grows more chili peppers than any other State.

New Orleans is famous for its fish and seafood, most notably pompano, trout, oysters, crawfish, crabs and shrimp, but also is the home of wonderfully exhilarating dishes of meat, chicken and game. In general it is Creole food that is eaten in the city of New Orleans, while the Cajun specialties come from the outlying districts. Cajun food is generally rough edged and hot – this is the land of Tabasco sauce and pepper-eating contests. A famous Cajun threesome is cayenne, black and white pepper, which are added in large amounts to soups and stews. Creole cooking is more refined and less fiery, but nevertheless uses lots of tomatoes, onions, garlic and red and green peppers and green herbs. Dip into New Orleans cooking, but beware – it's exciting!

Right: the elegant plantation houses on Charles Avenue, in the Garden District of
New Orleans, were built in the classic antebellum style.

Shrimp Bisque

Preparation Time: 20 minutes **Cooking Time:** 8-10 minutes **Serves:** 6

This classic Cajun recipe makes a first course or a full meal. It isn't a smooth purée like its French counterpart.

Ingredients

3 tbsps butter or margarine
1 onion, finely chopped
1 red pepper, finely chopped
2 celery stalks, finely chopped
1 clove garlic, minced
Pinch dry mustard and cayenne
  pepper

2 tsps paprika
3 tbsps all-purpose flour
4 cups fish stock
1 sprig thyme and bay leaf
8 oz raw, peeled shrimp
Salt and pepper
Snipped chives

Melt the butter or margarine in a large saucepan and add the onion, pepper, celery and garlic. Cook gently to soften. Stir in the mustard and cayenne, paprika and flour. Cook for about 3 minutes over low heat, stirring occasionally. Pour on the stock gradually, stirring until well blended. Add the thyme and bay leaf and bring to a boil. Reduce the heat and simmer for about 5 minutes or until thickened, stirring occasionally. Add the shrimp and cook for about 5 minutes, until pink and curled. Season with salt and pepper to taste. Serve, topped with snipped chives.

The best way to see the French Quarter of New Orleans with its narrow streets and cast-iron balconies, known as galleries, is by buggy or on foot.

Oeufs Marchand de Vin

Preparation Time: 45 minutes **Cooking Time:** 20-25 minutes **Serves:** 4

This is a classic egg dish from New Orleans served for brunch – the meal that's too late for breakfast but too early for lunch!

Ingredients

Full quantity Hollandaise sauce from the recipe for Eggs Sardou
4 eggs
4 slices smoked bacon
1 beefsteak tomato, thickly sliced
4 slices bread
Oil

½ small onion, finely chopped
1½ tbsps flour
1 clove garlic, crushed
6 mushrooms, finely chopped
¾ cup brown stock
6 tbsps red wine
Salt and pepper

Marchand de Vin Sauce

3 tbsps oil

Heat the oil for the Marchand de Vin sauce. Add the onion and cook until softened. Add the flour and cook slowly stirring frequently, until golden brown. Add the garlic and mushrooms and pour in the stock, stirring to blend well. Add the wine and bring the sauce to a boil. Lower the heat and simmer for about 15-20 minutes, stirring occasionally. Season to taste.

Poach the eggs according to the recipe for Eggs Sardou and place in cold water until ready to use.

Fry the bacon in a small amount of oil, or broil until crisp. Drain, crumble and set aside. Cut the bread with a cookie cutter into 3-inch diameter circles. Fry until golden brown and crisp in enough oil to just cover. Drain on paper towels and place on a serving plate. Spoon some of the Marchand de Vin sauce on top and keep warm in the oven. Place one tomato slice on top of the sauce on each bread crouton and continue to keep warm.

Reheat the eggs and drain well. Place one egg on top of each tomato slice. Spoon over some of the Hollandaise sauce and sprinkle with the bacon to serve.

Oysters Rockefeller

Preparation Time: about 25 minutes **Cooking Time:** 25 minutes **Serves:** 4

Oysters can be purchased already opened, and you'll find the rest of this famous New Orleans dish simplicity itself to prepare.

Ingredients

24 oysters on the half shell
Rock salt
6 strips bacon, finely chopped
1¼ lb fresh spinach, well washed, stems removed and leaves finely chopped
1 small bunch green onions, finely chopped

2 cloves garlic, crushed
4-5 tbsps fine fresh bread crumbs
Dash Tabasco
2 tbsps anisette liqueur
Pinch salt
Parmesan cheese

Remove the oysters from their shells, strain and reserve their liquid. Rinse the shells well and return an oyster to each one. Pour about 1 inch of rock salt into a baking pan and place in the oysters in their shells, pressing each shell gently into the salt.

Place the bacon in a large frying pan and cook slowly to render the fat. Turn up the heat and brown the bacon evenly. Add the spinach, green onions and garlic and cook slowly until softened. Add the bread crumbs, Tabasco, oyster liquid, liqueur, and a pinch of salt. Spoon some of the mixture onto each oyster and sprinkle with Parmesan cheese. Place in a preheated 350°F oven for about 15 minutes. Alternatively, heat through in the oven for 10 minutes and place under a preheated broiler to brown the cheese lightly. Serve immediately.

Top: many people still visit New Orleans just for its jazz clubs. Louis Armstrong, born in New Orleans in 1900, was the founder of jazz in the city.

Chicken and Shrimp Peppers

Preparation Time: 30 minutes **Cooking Time:** about 45-50 minutes **Serves:** 6

Peppers feature prominently in Creole cooking, either as a colorful addition or as a major part of a recipe like this one.

Ingredients

3 large green or red peppers
¼ cup butter or margarine
1 small onion, finely chopped
1 celery stalk, finely chopped
1 clove garlic, crushed
2 boneless chicken breasts, skinned and finely diced
4 oz cooked, peeled shrimp

2 tsps chopped parsley
Salt, pepper and a pinch cayenne pepper
½ loaf stale French bread, made into crumbs
1-2 eggs, beaten
6 tsps dry bread crumbs

Cut the peppers in half lengthwise and remove the cores and seeds. Leave the stems attached, if desired. Melt the butter in a frying pan and add the onion, celery, garlic and chicken. Cook over moderate heat until the vegetables are softened and the chicken is cooked. Add the shrimp and parsley. Season with salt, pepper and cayenne. Stir in the French bread crumbs and add enough beaten egg to make the mixture hold together.

Spoon filling into each pepper half, mounding the top slightly. Place the peppers in a baking dish that holds them closely together. Pour enough water down the side of the dish to come about ½ inch up the sides of the peppers. Cover and bake in a pre-heated 350°F oven for about 45 minutes, or until the peppers are just tender. Sprinkle each with the dried bread crumbs and place under a preheated broiler until golden brown. Serve hot or cold.

Eggs Sardou

Preparation Time: about 45 minutes **Cooking Time:** 20-25 minutes **Serves:** 4

A traditional New Orleans brunch dish, this can double as an appetizer or light supper dish, too.

Ingredients

1½ lbs fresh spinach	**Hollandaise Sauce**
1½ tbsps butter or margarine	3 egg yolks
1 tbsp flour	Pinch salt and pepper
1 cup milk	1 tbsp lemon juice
Salt, pepper and nutmeg	1 cup unsalted butter
4 artichoke hearts, quartered	1 large piece canned pimento, drained
4 eggs	and cut into 8 thin strips

Strip the spinach leaves from the stalks and wash the leaves well. Place the leaves in a large saucepan and add a pinch of salt. Cover the pan and cook the spinach over moderate heat in only the water that clings to the leaves. Do not add more water. When the spinach is just wilted, take off the heat and drain well. Chop roughly and set aside.

Melt the butter or margarine in a medium-sized sauce pan and stir in the flour. Gradually add the milk, beating constantly, and place the sauce over low heat. Beat the sauce as it comes to a boil and allow it to boil rapidly for about a minute to thicken. Stir in the spinach and season the sauce with salt, pepper and nutmeg. Add the artichoke hearts and set the sauce aside.

Fill a large frying pan with water and bring to a boil. Turn down the heat and, when the water is just barely simmering, break an egg into a cup or onto a saucer. Gently lower the egg into the water to poach. Repeat with the remaining eggs. Poach over a gentle heat, never allowing the water to boil. Alternatively, cook in a special poaching pan. Cook until the whites have set but the yolks are still soft. Remove the eggs from the pan with a slotted spoon and place in cold water until ready to use.

Place the egg yolks in a food processor or blender with the seasoning and lemon juice. Process once or twice to mix. Place the butter in a small saucepan and melt over gentle heat. Turn up the heat and when the butter is bubbling, take off the heat. With the machine running, gradually pour the butter onto the eggs in a very thin but steady stream.

To assemble the dish, reheat the spinach sauce and place an equal amount of it on each plate. Make a well in center. Place the eggs back into hot water briefly to reheat, and drain well. Place an egg in the hollow of the spinach sauce on each plate. Spoon over some of the Hollandaise sauce to coat each egg completely. Make a cross with two strips of pimento on top of each egg and serve immediately.

Coush-Coush

Preparation Time: 15 minutes **Cooking Time:** 20-25 minutes **Serves:** 4-6

Cornmeal is a favorite in the South, as a bread, a coating for frying or a warming breakfast meal.

Ingredients
1½ cups yellow cornmeal
4 tbsps all-purpose flour
1 tbsp baking powder
2 tsps sugar

Pinch salt
2½ cups water
⅓ cup butter or margarine

Mix the cornmeal and the other dry ingredients in a large bowl and add the water gradually, mixing until smooth. Melt the butter in a medium frying pan and, when foaming, add the cornmeal mixture, spreading it out smoothly in the pan. Turn up the heat and cook until brown and crisp on the bottom. Stir the mixture to distribute the brown crust. Reduce the heat and cover the pan tightly. Cook the mixture for about 10-15 minutes, stirring occasionally. Spoon into serving bowls and serve hot.

Top: Mardi Gras is the year's most anticipated event in New Orleans with its colorful parades and street dancing.

Shellfish Boil

Preparation Time: 30 minutes **Cooking Time:** about 35 minutes **Serves:** 4-6

This is the Cajun way to cook seafood. Drained seafood is piled onto newspaper-covered tables for everyone to dig in.

Ingredients

3 quarts water
1 lemon, quartered
1 onion, cut in half but not peeled
1 celery stalk, cut in 3 pieces
2 cloves garlic, left whole
Pinch salt
4 dried bay leaves, finely crumbled
4 dried red chili peppers, crumbled

1 tbsp each whole cloves, whole
  allspice, coriander seed and
  mustard seed
2 tsps celery seed
1 tbsp dill weed, fresh or ½ tsp dried
1 lb raw, unpeeled shrimp
2 lbs mussels, well scrubbed

Place the water, lemon, onion, celery, garlic, salt, bay leaves, chili peppers, spices, and dill weed together in a large pot and cover. Bring to a boil, reduce the heat and cook slowly for 20 minutes. Add the shrimp in two batches and cook for about 5 minutes, until pink and curled. Remove with a slotted spoon.

  Add mussels to the pot and cook, stirring frequently, for about 5 minutes or until shells have opened. Discard any that do not open. Spoon shrimp and mussels into serving bowls and serve immediately.

Steamboat House in New Orleans is a monument celebrating the city's great
Mississippi river.

Hot Pepper Egg Salad

Preparation Time: 25 minutes **Cooking Time:** 9 minutes **Serves:** 4-6

Cajun cooks excel at using what is on hand, and this salad is made with just those kinds of ingredients.

Ingredients

4 eggs
Half a bunch of green onions, chopped
½ small red pepper, chopped
½ small green pepper, chopped
4 oz cooked, peeled shrimp
1 small jar or can artichoke hearts, drained and quartered

Dressing
6 tbsps oil
2 tbsps white wine vinegar
1 clove garlic, finely chopped
1 tsp dry mustard
1-2 tsps hot red pepper flakes, or 1 small fresh chili, seeded and finely chopped
Salt

Prick the large end of the eggs with an egg pricker or a needle. Lower each egg carefully into boiling, salted water. Bring the water back to a boil, rolling the eggs in the water with the bowl of a spoon and cook the eggs for 9 minutes. Drain and rinse under cold water until completely cool. Peel and quarter. Combine the eggs with the other salad ingredients in a large bowl.

Mix the dressing ingredients together using a beater to get a thick consistency. Pour the dressing over the salad and mix carefully so that the eggs do not break up. Serve on beds of shredded lettuce, if desired.

Oak Alley, Vacherie, west of New Orleans, was acquired by a sugar planter in 1837. He built the Greek Revival house with 28 columns to echo the 28-tree canopy.

Crabmeat Imperial

Preparation Time: 45 minutes **Cooking Time:** 10 minutes **Serves:** 2-4

Another of New Orleans' famous dishes, this makes a delicious warm weather salad for lunches, light suppers or elegant appetizers.

Ingredients

2 small crabs, boiled
2 tbsps oil
4 green onions
1 small green pepper, seeded and finely chopped
1 celery stalk, finely chopped
1 clove garlic, crushed
¾ cup mayonnaise
1 tbsp mild mustard

Dash Tabasco and Worcestershire sauce
1 piece canned pimiento, drained and finely chopped
2 tbsps chopped parsley
Salt and pepper
Lettuce, curly endive or raddichio (optional)

To shell the crabs, first remove all the legs and the large claws by twisting and pulling them away from the body. Turn the shell over and, using your thumbs, push the body away from the flat shell. Set the body aside. Remove the stomach sack and the lungs, (dead man's fingers) and discard them. Using a small teaspoon, scrape the brown body meat out of the flat shell and reserve. Using a sharp knife, cut the body of the crab in four pieces and, using a pick or a skewer, push out all the meat. Crack the large claws and remove the meat in one piece if possible. Crack the larger legs and remove that meat as well. Set all the meat aside. Scrub the shells if desired to use for serving.

Heat the oil in a small frying pan. Chop the white parts of the green onions and add to the oil with the green pepper, celery and garlic. Cook over gentle heat for about 10 minutes, stirring often, to soften the vegetables but not brown them. Remove from the heat and set aside. When cool, add the mayonnaise, mustard, Tabasco and Worcestershire sauce, pimiento and finely chopped tops of the green onions. Spoon the reserved brown body meat from the crabs back into each shell or serving dish. Mix the remaining crabmeat with the dressing, reserving the crab claws for garnish, if desired, or shred and add to the other crabmeat. Do not overmix the sauce as the crabmeat should stay in large pieces. Spoon into the shells on top of the brown body meat, sprinkle with chopped parsley and place the crab shells on serving plates, surrounding them with lettuce leaves, if desired. Garnish with the shelled crab claws or use the crab legs. Serve immediately.

Red Beans and Rice

Preparation Time: about 25 minutes plus overnight soaking
Cooking Time: 2½-3 hours **Serves:** 6-8

Served every Monday in New Orleans, this is a delicious way of making a small amount of meat go a long way.

Ingredients

8 oz dried red kidney beans
1 sprig thyme
1 bay leaf
8 oz ham or bacon
¼ cup butter or margarine
1 onion, finely chopped
1 green pepper, finely diced

2 cloves garlic, crushed
3 celery stalks, finely chopped
1 tsp cayenne pepper
Salt
8 oz rice, cooked
4 green onions, finely chopped

Pick over the beans and place them in a large stockpot or bowl. Cover with water and let soak overnight. Drain them and place in a pan of fresh water with the sprig of thyme, bay leaf and a pinch of salt. Add the piece of ham or bacon and bring to a boil. Partially cover the pan and let boil rapidly for 10 minutes. Reduce the heat and then simmer for 2½-3 hours, adding more water if necessary.

When the beans have been cooking for about half the required length of time, melt the butter in a small frying pan and cook the onion, pepper, garlic and celery until the onions look translucent. Add this mixture to the beans and continue cooking them. Once the beans are soft, mash some of them against the side of the pan with a large spoon. Or, remove about ¾ cup of the mixture and blend to a smooth purée in a food processor or blender. Pour back into the pan to thicken the rest of the beans.

Next remove the piece of ham or bacon, trim off excess fat and cut the meat into ½-inch pieces. Return to the beans and add cayenne pepper. Stir well and continue to cook the beans. Remove thyme and bay leaf before serving. To serve, place rice on serving plates and spoon some of the beans over the rice. Sprinkle the top with the chopped green onion.

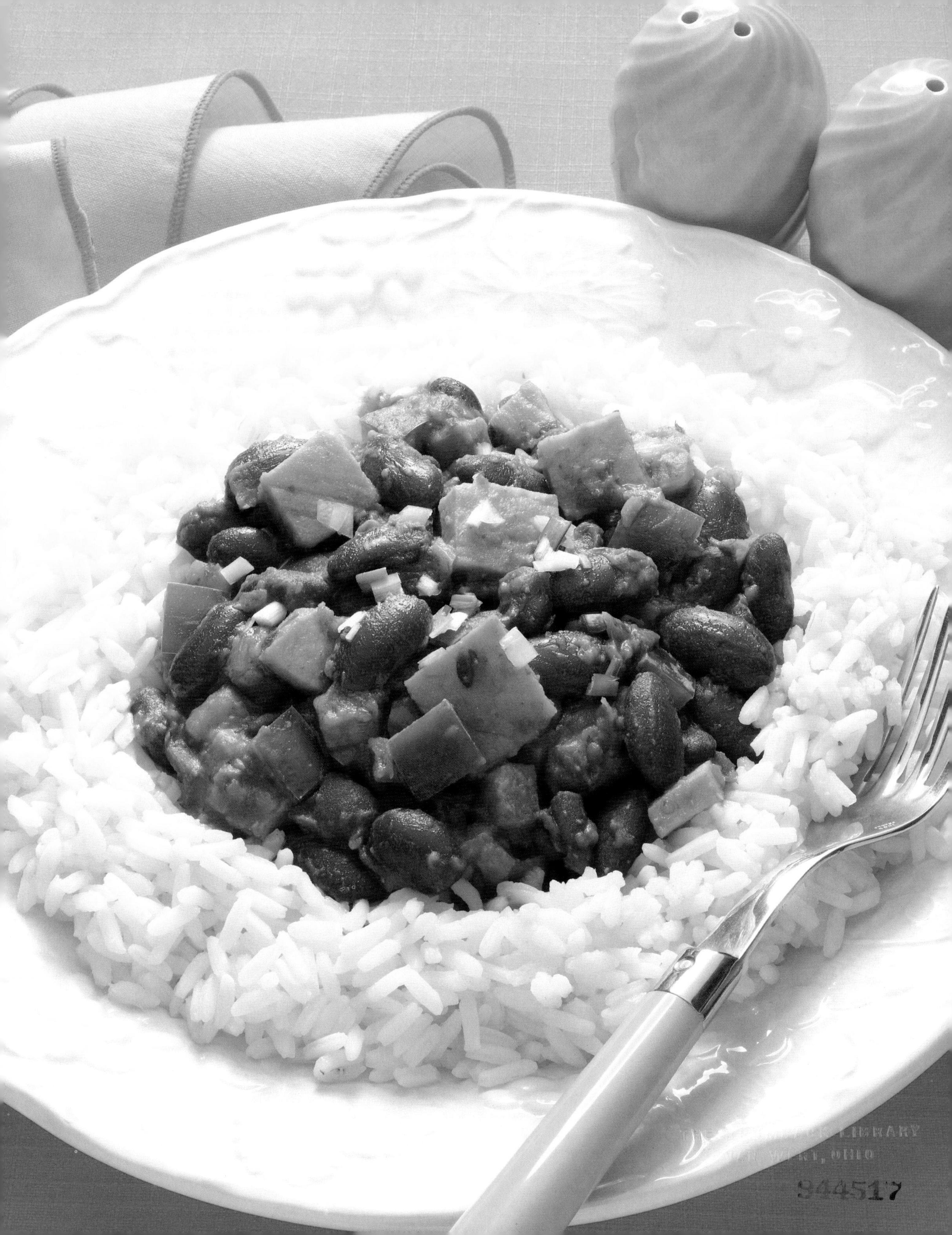

Shrimp Creole

Preparation Time: 25 minutes **Cooking Time:** 20-30 minutes **Serves:** 4

Deceptively simple, this dish combines all the ingredients that characterize Creole cooking – seafood, garlic, tomatoes, peppers, herbs, and a dash of hot pepper.

Ingredients

4 tbsps oil
1 large green pepper, seeded and
  cut into 1-inch pieces
2 celery stalks, sliced
2 medium onions, diced
2 cloves garlic, crushed
2 x 14 oz cans tomatoes
2 bay leaves

1 tsp cayenne pepper or Tabasco
  sauce
Pinch salt and pepper
Pinch thyme
2 tbsps cornstarch mixed with 3 tbsps
  dry white wine
1½ lb shrimp, uncooked
4 oz rice, cooked

Place the oil in a large saucepan and add the vegetables. Cook for a few minutes over low heat and add the garlic. Add the tomatoes and their juice, breaking up the tomatoes with a fork or a potato masher. Add the bay leaves, cayenne pepper or Tabasco, seasoning and thyme, and bring to a boil. Allow to simmer for about 5 minutes, uncovered. Mix a few spoonfuls of the hot tomato liquid with the cornstarch mixture and then return it to the saucepan. Bring to a boil, stirring constantly until thickened. Add the shrimp and cover the pan. Simmer over low heat for about 20 minutes, or until the shrimp curl and look pink and opaque. Remove the bay leaves before serving, and spoon the sauce over rice.

Diesel-powered replicas of the original sternwheeler steamboats offer excursions into Louisiana's Bayou country to the south and west of New Orleans.

Chicken St. Pierre

Preparation Time: 35 minutes **Cooking Time:** about 40 minutes **Serves:** 4-6

A French name for a very Southern combination of chicken, lima beans, peppers and onions made into a spicy, aromatic stew.

Ingredients

⅔ cup butter or margarine
3 lb chicken, cut in 8 pieces
3 tbsps flour
1 large red pepper, diced
1 large green pepper, diced
6 green onions, chopped

½ cup dry white wine
1 cup chicken stock
6 oz lima beans
1 tsp chopped thyme or ½ tsp dried
Salt, pepper and pinch nutmeg
Dash Tabasco (optional)

Heat the butter in a large frying pan and when foaming, add the chicken, skin side down. Brown on one side, turn over and brown the other side. Remove the chicken and add the flour to the pan. Cook to a pale straw color. Add the peppers and onions and cook briefly. Pour on the wine and chicken stock and bring to a boil. Stir constantly until thickened. Add the chicken, lima beans, thyme, seasoning and nutmeg. Cover the pan and cook about 25 minutes, or until the chicken is tender. Add Tabasco to taste, if desired, before serving.

Top: St. Louis Cathedral, grandly presiding over Jackson Square, New Orleans, is built in the Spanish style and dates from 1789.

Paneed Lemon Veal

Preparation Time: 25 minutes **Cooking Time:** 20-25 minutes **Serves:** 4

Paneed means pan-fried in Creole – a perfect way to prepare this tender cut of veal that only needs brief cooking.

Ingredients

8 veal cutlets
Flour
Salt and pepper
2 tbsps butter or margarine
1 green pepper, thinly sliced

6 tbsps dry white wine
1 tbsp lemon juice
¾ cup chicken stock
1 lemon, peeled and thinly sliced

Sprinkle the veal with a mixture of flour, and salt and pepper. Shake off the excess. Melt the butter or margarine in a large frying pan and brown the veal, a few pieces at a time. Remove the meat and keep it warm. Cook the peppers briefly and set aside with the veal. Pour the wine and lemon juice into the pan to deglaze. Add the stock and bring to a boil. Boil for 5 minutes to reduce. Add the veal and peppers and cook for 15 minutes over gentle heat. Add the lemon slices and heat through before serving.

The fantastic spectacle of the Mardi Gras carnival attracts tourists from all over the world who come to enjoy all the color and spectacle the city's most famous event.

Poisson en Papillote

Preparation Time: 40 minutes **Cooking Time:** about 20 minutes **Serves:** 4

A famous New Orleans dish that cannot fail to impress at a special dinner party, this recipe demands the use of freshly prepared fish stock.

Ingredients

8 single or 4 double whitefish fillets
Fish bones and trimmings
1 bay leaf, sprig thyme and
   2 parsley stalks
6 black peppercorns
1 slice lemon
1 cup dry white wine
1 cup water

8 large uncooked shrimp, shelled
4 crab claws, cracked and shelled
¼ cup butter or margarine
3 tbsps flour
1 onion, finely chopped
Pinch salt and pepper
2 egg yolks

Preheat the oven to 400°F. To make fish stock, skin the fish fillets and place the skin in a large stockpot along with the fish bones, bay leaf, thyme, parsley stalks, peppercorns and lemon slice. Add the wine and water and bring to a boil. Lower the heat and simmer for 20 minutes. Strain and set aside.

Cut wax paper into large ovals big enough to form a packet for each fish fillet. Fold the paper in half and lightly oil both sides. Place the fish fillets on one half of the paper and arrange the shrimp and crab claws on top of each fillet.

Melt the butter in a heavy-bottomed saucepan and, when foaming, add the flour. Cook over moderate heat for 2-3 minutes, stirring frequently until a pale straw color. Add the onion and cook until lightly browned. Gradually pour in the fish stock, beating continuously. Cook over moderate heat for about 4-5 minutes, or until the sauce thickens.

Mix the egg yolks with a few spoonfuls of the hot sauce and then stir the egg yolks into the sauce. Spoon some of the sauce over each fillet and seal the packets, folding the edge over twice and twisting the ends slightly to seal completely. Place the parcels on cookie sheets or in shallow baking pans and place in a preheated oven for about 20 minutes. Serve the packets unopened, to be opened at the table. Serve any remaining sauce separately.

Seafood Gumbo Filé

Preparation Time: 25-30 minutes **Cooking Time:** 20-25 minutes **Serves:** 6

Either filé powder, made from sassafras leaves, or okra gives a Cajun gumbo its characteristic texture.

Ingredients

1 lb cooked, unpeeled shrimp
Half quantity spice mixture (see
   Shellfish Boil)
5 cups water
4 tbsps butter or margarine
1 onion, sliced
1 green pepper, sliced
2 cloves garlic, finely chopped
3 tbsps all-purpose flour

½ tsp fresh thyme or ¼ tsp dried
1 bay leaf
2 tbsps chopped parsley
Dash Worcestershire sauce
12 oysters, shelled
8 oz tomatoes, peeled and chopped
2 tbsps filé powder (optional)
Salt and pepper
Cooked rice

Peel the shrimp and reserve the shells. Mix shells with the spice mixture and water and bring to a boil in a large stock pot. Reduce the heat and allow to simmer for about 20 minutes.

Melt the butter or margarine and, when foaming, add the onion, green pepper, garlic and flour. Cook slowly, stirring constantly until the flour is a pale golden brown. Gradually strain the stock, discarding the shells and spice mixture, into the flour, onions and spices. Add the thyme and bay leaf and stir well. Bring to a boil and then simmer until thick.

Add the parsley and the Worcestershire sauce to taste. Add the oysters, peeled shrimp and tomatoes and heat through gently to cook the oysters. Stir in the filé powder and let stand to thicken. Adjust the seasoning and serve over rice.

Fried Chicken Creole

Preparation Time: about 25 minutes **Cooking Time:** 30-40 minutes **Serves:** 6

Not the usual crisp Southern-style fried chicken, this is cooked in a tomato sauce flavored with garlic, herbs and wine.

Ingredients

Flour for dredging
Salt and pepper
3 lb frying chicken, cut in 8 pieces
6 tbsps oil
5 tbsps butter or margarine
1 clove garlic, crushed
1 small onion, finely chopped

4 oz bacon or uncooked ham, diced
6 tomatoes, peeled and chopped
2 tsps fresh thyme or 1 tsp dried thyme
Salt and pepper
½ cup white wine
2 tbsps chopped parsley

Mix the flour with salt and pepper and sprinkle lightly over the chicken, shaking the pieces to remove any excess flour. Heat the oil in a large frying pan and, when hot, add the butter. Add the chicken pieces, skin side down, and allow to brown over a moderately low heat so that the chicken cooks as well as browns. Turn the pieces over and brown on the other side. Cook in two batches if necessary. Add the garlic, onion and bacon or ham to the pan and lower the heat. Cook slowly for about 10 minutes, or until the bacon browns slightly. Add the tomatoes, thyme and seasoning and lower the heat. Cook until the chicken is just tender and the tomatoes are softened.

　　Using a slotted spoon, transfer the chicken and other ingredients to a serving dish and keep warm. Remove all but about 4 tbsps of the fat from the pan and deglaze with the wine, scraping up the browned bits from the bottom. Bring to a boil and allow to reduce slightly. To serve, pour the wine over the chicken and then sprinkle with chopped parsley.

Trout with Oyster Stuffing

Preparation Time: 30 minutes **Cooking Time:** 30 minutes **Serves:** 4

Oysters are used freely in Cajun cooking since they are plentiful in this part of the world. They make a luxurious stuffing for whole fish.

Ingredients

4 whole trout, about 8 oz each, cleaned
½ cup butter or margarine
1 onion, finely chopped
2 celery stalks, finely chopped
1 small red pepper, finely chopped
4 green onions, finely chopped
1 clove garlic, crushed
12 oysters on the half shell
¼ tsp white pepper
¼ tsp cayenne pepper
¼ tsp black pepper
2 tsps chopped parsley
1 tsp chopped fresh dill
1 cup dry bread crumbs
2 small eggs, lightly beaten
Pinch salt

Wash the trout well inside and pat dry. Melt half the butter or margarine in a medium saucepan. Add onion, celery, red pepper, green onions and garlic. Cook over moderate heat for about 3 minutes to soften the vegetables.

Remove the oysters from the shells with a sharp knife. Strain and reserve the liquid. Add the oysters to the vegetables and cook for about 2 minutes, breaking the oysters up into large pieces. Stir in the white pepper, cayenne pepper and black pepper, dill and parsley.

Remove from heat, add the bread crumbs and gradually beat in the egg, adding just enough to hold the stuffing ingredients together. Season with salt. Stuff the cavity of each trout with an equal amount of the stuffing and place the trout in a baking dish. Spoon the remaining butter over the trout and bake, uncovered, in a preheated 350°F oven for about 25 minutes. Brown under a preheated broiler before serving, if desired.

Crawfish Pie

Preparation Time: 30 minutes **Cooking Time:** 10 minutes for the filling and 25 minutes to finish the dish **Serves:** 4

This seafood, plentiful in southern Louisiana, is used in many delicious ways. The boiling mixture adds spice, and the browned flour a nutty taste and good color.

Ingredients

Pastry	Filling
2 cups all-purpose flour	3 tbsps oil
Pinch salt	3 tbsps flour
½-¾ cup butter or margarine	½ green pepper, finely diced
Cold water	2 green onions, finely chopped
½ quantity spice mixture for	1 celery stalk, finely chopped
Shellfish Boil (see recipe)	1 cup light cream
1 lb raw, shelled crawfish or shrimp	Salt and pepper

Sift the flour into a bowl with a pinch of salt and cut in the butter or margarine until the mixture resembles fine bread crumbs. Add enough cold water to bring the mixture together. Knead into a ball, wrap well and chill for about 30 minutes before use.

Combine the spice mixture with about 2½ cups water. Bring to a boil and add the crawfish or shrimp. Cook for about 5 minutes, stirring occasionally until the shellfish curl up. Remove from the liquid and let drain.

Heat the oil in a small saucepan and add the flour. Cook slowly, stirring constantly until the flour turns a rich dark brown. Add the remaining filling ingredients, stirring constantly while adding the cream. Bring to a boil, reduce the heat and cook for about 5 minutes. Add the crawfish or shrimp to the sauce.

Divide the pastry into 4 portions and roll out each portion on a lightly-floured surface to about ¼-inch thick. Line individual flan or pie dishes with the pastry, pushing it carefully onto the bottom and down the sides, taking care not to stretch it. Trim off excess pastry and reserve.

Place a sheet of wax paper or foil on the pastry and pour on rice, pasta or baking beans until they come halfway up the sides. Bake the pastry for about 10 minutes in a preheated 400°F oven. Remove the paper and beans and bake for an additional 5 minutes to cook the base.

Spoon in the filling and roll out any trimmings to make a lattice pattern on top. Bake another 10 minutes to brown the lattice and heat the filling. Cool slightly before serving.

Backbone Stew

Preparation Time: 25 minutes **Cooking Time:** 1½-2 hours **Serves:** 8

A mixture of three kinds of pepper is typically Cajun. Normally made with pork, this stew is also good with inexpensive cuts of lamb.

Ingredients

3 lb middle neck or other neck cut
  of lamb
¼ tsp each cayenne, white and
  black pepper
Pinch salt
6 tbsps oil
2 onions, sliced

1 large red pepper, sliced
2 celery stalks, sliced
6 tbsps flour
2 cloves garlic, crushed
5 cups stock or water
2 tbsps chopped parsley

Cut the lamb between the bones into individual pieces. Sprinkle a mixture of red, white and black pepper and salt over the surface of the chops, patting it in well. Heat the oil in a large stock pot or casserole and when hot, add the meat, a few pieces at a time, and brown on both sides. When all the meat is brown, remove from stock pot or casserole to a plate and add the onions, pepper and celery to the oil. Lower the heat and cook to soften. Remove and set aside with the meat. Add the flour to the remaining oil in the pan and stir well. Cook slowly until a dark golden brown. Add the garlic and stir in the stock or water. Return the meat and vegetables to the pan or casserole and bring to a boil. Cover and cook slowly for 1½-2 hours, or until the lamb is very tender. Sprinkle with parsley and serve immediately.

LaFitte's Blacksmith Shop in the French Quarter of New Orleans, dating from 1772, was built in the indigenous style using sturdy cypress timbers to support the bricks.

Pigeons in Wine

Preparation Time: 30 minutes **Cooking Time:** 50 minutes-1 hour **Serves:** 4

Pigeons are country fare and these are treated in a provinical French manner with the Cajun touch of white, black and red pepper.

Ingredients

4 pigeons
½ tsp each cayenne, white and
    black pepper
Pinch salt
2 tbsps oil
2 tbsps butter or margarine
12 oz button onions
2 celery stalks, sliced
4 carrots, sliced

4 tbsps flour
1½ cups chicken stock
½ cup dry red wine
2 tsps tomato paste (optional)
4 oz button mushrooms, quartered or
    left whole if small
3 oz fresh or frozen lima beans
2 tbsps chopped parsley

Wipe the pigeons with a damp cloth and season the cavities with the three kinds of pepper and pinch of salt. Heat the oil in a large heavy-bottomed pan and add the butter or margarine. Once it is foaming, place in the pigeons, two at a time if necessary, and brown them on all sides, turning them frequently. Remove from the pan and set them aside.

To peel the button onions quickly, trim the root ends slightly and drop the onions into rapidly boiling water. Allow it to come back to the boil for about 1 minute. Transfer to cold water and leave to cool completely. The skins should come off easily. Trim roots completely.

Add the onions, celery and carrots to the pan and cook for about 5 minutes to brown slightly. Add the flour and cook until golden brown, stirring constantly. Pour in the stock and the wine and stir well. Bring to a boil over high heat until thickened.

Stir in the tomato paste, if using, and return the pigeons to the pan along with any liquid that has accumulated. Partially cover the casserole and simmer gently for about 40-45 minutes, or until the pigeons are tender. Add the mushrooms and lima beans halfway through the cooking time. To serve, skim any excess fat from the surface of the sauce and sprinkle the chopped parsley over the top.

New Orleans Jambalaya

Preparation Time: 40 minutes **Cooking Time** 25-30 minutes **Serves:** 4-6

An easy and extremely satisfying dish of rice and seafood. Sometimes garlic sausage is added for extra spice.

Ingredients
2 tbsps butter or margarine
2 tbsps all-purpose flour
1 medium onion, finely chopped
1 clove garlic, crushed
1 red pepper, finely chopped
14 oz canned tomatoes
4 cups fish or chicken stock
¼ tsp ground ginger
Pinch allspice

1 tsp chopped fresh thyme or
    ½ tsp dried thyme
¼ tsp cayenne pepper
Pinch salt
Dash Tabasco
4 oz uncooked rice
2 lbs uncooked shrimp, peeled
2 green onions, chopped, for garnish

Melt the butter in a heavy-bottomed saucepan and then add the flour. Stir to blend well and cook over low heat until a pale straw color. Add the onion, garlic and pepper and cook until soft. Add the tomatoes and their juice, breaking up the tomatoes with a fork or a potato masher. Add the stock and mix well. Add the ginger, allspice, thyme, cayenne pepper, salt and Tabasco. Bring to a boil and allow to boil rapidly, stirring, for about 2 minutes. Add the rice, stir well and cover the pan. Cook for about 15-20 minutes, or until the rice is tender and has absorbed most of the liquid. Add the shrimp during the last 10 minutes of cooking time. Cook until the shrimp curl and turn pink. Adjust the seasoning, spoon into a serving dish and sprinkle with the chopped green onion to serve.

Braised Rabbit with Peppers

Preparation Time: 25 minutes, plus overnight soaking
Cooking Time: 50 minutes - 1 hour **Serves:** 4

Rabbit was a staple in the diets of the early Cajun settlers, who used local ingredients to vary this classic French game stew.

Ingredients

2¼ lb rabbit joints
1 lemon slice
Flour for dredging
1 tsp dry mustard
1 tsp paprika
¼ tsp each cayenne, white and
   black pepper
1 tsp garlic powder
¼ tsp dried dill

Pinch salt and pepper
Oil
1 onion, thinly sliced
1 small green pepper, thinly sliced
1 small red pepper, thinly sliced
14 oz canned tomatoes
1 cup chicken stock
1 bay leaf
4 tbsps dry white wine

Soak the rabbit overnight with the lemon slice in cold water to cover. Drain the rabbit and pat dry with paper towels. Combine flour, spices, herbs and seasoning and sprinkle the rabbit with the mixture.

   Heat the oil and fry the rabbit on all sides until golden brown. Remove to a plate. Cook the onion and peppers for about a minute. Add the tomatoes, stock and bay leaf and bring to a boil. Return the rabbit to the pan and spoon the sauce over the rabbit. Partially cover and cook for about 45-50 minutes over a gentle heat until tender. Add the wine during the last 10 minutes of cooking. Remove the bay leaf before serving.

Creole Tomatoes

Preparation Time: about 30 minutes **Cooking Time:** 15-20 minutes **Serves:** 4

A perfect side dish for grilled chicken or fish, this is especially good for summer, when tomatoes are at their best.

Ingredients

4 large ripe tomatoes
1 small green pepper, thinly sliced
4 green onions, sliced
1 clove garlic, crushed

4 tbsps white wine
Pinch cayenne pepper and salt
1 tbsp butter or margarine
4 tbsps heavy cream

Place tomatoes in a pan of boiling water, leave for 30 seconds and remove with a slotted spoon. Place immediately in a bowl of ice cold water.

Use a small, sharp knife to remove the peel, beginning at the stem end. Cut the tomatoes in half and scoop out the seeds. Strain the juice and reserve it, discarding the seeds. Place tomatoes cut side down in a baking dish and sprinkle the reserved juice over them. Add the sliced pepper, onions, garlic, wine, cayenne pepper and salt. Dot with butter or margarine.

Place in a preheated 350°F oven for about 15-20 minutes, or until the tomatoes are heated through and are tender, but not falling apart. Strain juice into a small saucepan. Bring juice to a boil to reduce slightly. Stir in the cream and reboil. To serve, spoon the juice over the tomatoes.

Fanciful wrought ironwork balconies, or galleries, are one of the hallmarks of the beautifully preserved French Quarter in New Orleans.

Green Rice

Preparation Time: 20 minutes **Cooking Time:** 20-25 minutes **Serves:** 6

Fresh herbs are a must for this rice dish, but use whatever mixture suits your taste or complements the main course.

Ingredients
2 tbsps oil
2 tbsps butter
¾ cup uncooked long-grain rice
2 cups boiling water
Pinch salt and pepper

3 oz mixed, chopped fresh herbs
   e.g. parsley, thyme, marjoram, basil
1 small bunch green onions, finely
   chopped

Heat the oil in a large, heavy-bottomed saucepan and add the butter. When foaming, add the rice and cook over a moderate heat for about 2 minutes, stirring constantly. When the rice begins to look opaque, add the water and salt and pepper and bring to a boil, stirring occasionally. Cover the pan and reduce the heat. Simmer very gently, without stirring, for about 20 minutes or until all the liquid has been absorbed and the rice is tender. Chop the herbs very finely and stir into the rice along with the green onions. Cover the pan and let stand for 5 minutes before serving.

Top: replicas of the sternwheeler and sidewheeler steamboats take New Orleans visitors out on the Mississippi, either round the harbor or out into Bayou country.

Bread Pudding with Whiskey Sauce

Preparation Time: 40 minutes **Cooking Time** 35-40 minutes **Serves:** 8

A childhood pudding made sophisticated by the addition of a bourbon-laced sauce, and a stylish presentation.

Ingredients

½ loaf day-old French bread
2 cups milk
3 eggs
¾ cup raisins
1 tsp vanilla extract
Pinch ground ginger

Butter or margarine
½ cup butter
1 cup sugar
1 egg
4 tbsps bourbon
Nutmeg

Cut bread into small pieces and soak in the milk. When the bread has softened, add the eggs, raisins, vanilla and ginger. Grease 8 custard cups with butter or margarine and fill each with an equal amount of pudding mixture to within ½ inch of the top. Place the dishes in a roasting pan and pour in enough hot water to come halfway up the sides of the dishes. Bake in a preheated 350°F oven for about 35-40 minutes or until risen and set. When the puddings have cooked, combine the ½ cup butter and the sugar in the top of a double boiler and heat to dissolve the sugar.

Beat the egg and stir in a spoonful of the hot butter mixture. Add the egg to the double boiler and whip over a gentle heat until thick. Allow to cool and add bourbon. To serve, turn out puddings onto plates and surround with sauce. Sprinkle the tops with nutmeg.

Oak Alley Plantation House, west of New Orleans on the River Road, was built in the Greek Revival style by a sugar planter in 1837 for his new bride.

Beignets with Apricot Sauce

Preparation Time: 20 minutes **Cooking Time:** 2 minutes per batch **Serves:** 6

French in origin, these fritters are easier to make than the classic Creole type, but just as delicious.

Ingredients

6 tbsps water
1 tbsp butter or margarine
6 tbsps all-purpose flour
3-4 eggs
Few drops vanilla extract
Oil for deep-frying
Powdered sugar

Apricot Sauce
14 canned apricots, chopped
1 tbsp cornstarch mixed with
  4 tbsps bourbon
Dash lemon juice

Combine the water and butter or margarine in a saucepan and slowly bring to a boil. When boiling rapidly, quickly stir in the flour and remove the pan from the heat. Beat in the eggs one at a time, beating well in between each addition. It may not be necessary to add all the eggs. The mixture should be of dropping consistency and hold its shape well. Beat in the vanilla extract.

Heat the oil to 350°F in a deep fat fryer or in a deep saucepan on top of the stove. Drop the batter from a teaspoon into the hot fat and cook until puffed and golden. The beignets will rise to the surface of the oil when cooked and may be turned over if necessary. Cook about four beignets at a time. Drain on paper towels and sprinkle with powdered sugar.

While the beignets are cooking, combine all the sauce ingredients in a heavy-bottomed pan and bring to a boil. Cook until thickened and then transfer to a blender or food processor and purée until smooth. Serve immediately while the sauce and beignets are still warm.

Bananas Foster

Preparation Time: 15 minutes **Cooking Time:** 5 minutes **Serves:** 4

This rich concoction originated in a famous New Orleans restaurant, but it's now a favorite on any Creole menu.

Ingredients

4 ripe bananas, peeled
Juice of ½ lemon
½ cup butter
½ cup soft brown sugar, light or dark
Pinch ground cinnamon and nutmeg

4 tbsps orange juice
½ cup white or dark rum
Whipping cream
Chopped pecans

Cut the bananas in half lengthwise and sprinkle with lemon juice on all sides. Melt the butter in a large frying pan and add the sugar, cinnamon and nutmeg and orange juice. Stir over low heat until the sugar dissolves into a syrup. Add the banana halves and cook gently for about 3 minutes, basting the bananas often with syrup, but not turning them. Once the bananas are heated through, warm the rum in a small saucepan and ignite with a match. Pour the flaming rum over the bananas and shake the pan gently until the flames die down. Place 2 banana halves on each serving plate and top with some of the cream. Sprinkle with pecans and serve immediately.

The French Quarter of New Orleans, where the original colorful streets, courtyards and grillwork have all been lovingly preserved, covers only about a square mile.

Sweet Potato Pudding

Preparation Time: about 20 minutes **Cooking Time:** about 15-20 minutes for the sweet potatoes and 45 minutes for the pudding to bake **Serves:** 6

The sweet potato reigns supreme in Southern cooking, and this dish is satisfying either hot or cold.

Ingredients
1 lb sweet potatoes
1 cup butter
¾ cup white sugar
¾ cup light brown sugar
4 eggs
2 cups flour

1 tsp baking powder
½ tsp allspice
1 tsp ground nutmeg
½ tsp ground cinnamon
Pinch salt
⅔ cup milk

Peel the sweet potatoes, cut into cubes and place in boiling water deep enough to cover them. Cook until tender, drain and let dry completely. Cream the butter or margarine until light and fluffy and beat in the sugar gradually. Beat in the eggs one at a time, beating well in between each addition. Sift half the dry ingredients into the egg mixture and beat well. Add half the milk and then repeat with the remaining dry mixture and milk, beating well after each addition. Mash the sweet potatoes and add to the flour and egg mixture. Lightly butter a baking dish and spread in the sweet potato mixture. Smooth the top and bake in a preheated 375°F oven for about 45 minutes, or until top is firm to the touch. Allow to cool slightly before serving.

Mardi Gras Cakes

Preparation Time: 40 minutes, plus 1½-2 hours rising time
Cooking Time: 20-25 minutes **Makes:** 12

A different version of the King's cake, made to celebrate this famous Lenten carnival in New Orleans. The three colors symbolize justice, power and faith.

Ingredients

1 package dried active yeast
6 tbsps lukewarm water
2 tsps sugar
2 cups all-purpose flour
4 tbsps additional sugar
Pinch salt
1 tsp ground ginger
Grated rind 1 lemon
2 eggs
6 tbsps lukewarm milk
4 tbsps butter or margarine, cut in
    small pieces
4 oz golden raisins, currants and
    chopped, candied fruit, mixed

Icing
¾ cup granulated sugar
Purple, yellow and green food
    colorings
2 cups powdered sugar
Juice 1 lemon
Hot water

Sprinkle the yeast on top of the lukewarm water and stir in the sugar. Set in a warm place to prove for 15 minutes, or until bubbly. Sift the flour, sugar, salt and ginger into a large bowl and add the lemon rind. Make a well in the center of the ingredients and pour in the yeast. Add the egg and milk. Beat well, drawing the flour in from the outside edge, and gradually add the butter, a few pieces at a time. Turn the dough out onto a well-floured surface and knead for about 10 minutes, until smooth and elastic. Place the dough in a large, lightly-oiled bowl and cover with oiled plastic wrap. Let rise in a warm place for 1-1½ hours, or until doubled in bulk.

Punch the dough down and knead in the fruit to distribute it evenly. Oil a muffin tin with 12 spaces. Divide the dough into 12 and knead each piece into a smooth ball. Place a ball in each space in the tin and cover lightly. Leave in a warm place for 20-30 minutes to rise a second time. Bake at 375°F for about 20-25 minutes, or until golden brown. Allow to cool slightly and loosen the cakes. Cool completely before removing from the tin. Place an equal portion of sugar in each of three jars and add a drop of different food coloring to each. Shake the jars to color the sugar. Sift the powdered sugar and mix with the lemon juice. Add enough hot water to make an icing that pours easily but still clings to the back of a spoon. Spoon some icing over each cake and sprinkle the cakes with the different colored sugars before the icing sets.

Oreilles de Cochon

Preparation Time: 30 minutes **Cooking Time:** about 2 minutes per pastry
Makes: 12

These light, delicate pastries have a rather unusual name – Pig's Ears! It refers strictly to the shape the dough takes when deep fried.

Ingredients
1 cup all-purpose flour
1 tsp baking powder
¼ tsp salt
4 tbsps cold water

Oil for frying
1½ cups cane syrup mixed with
    ¾ cup molasses
3 oz finely chopped pecans

Sift the flour, baking powder and salt together in a large bowl. Make a well in the center and pour in the cold water. Using a wooden spoon, mix until a stiff dough forms, and then knead by hand until smooth. Divide the dough into 12 portions, each about the size of a walnut. Roll out each portion of dough on a floured surface until very thin. Heat the oil in a deep fat fryer to 350°F. Drop each piece of pastry into the hot fat using two forks. Twist the pastry just as it hits the oil. Cook one at a time until light brown. In a large saucepan, boil the syrup until it forms a soft ball when dropped into cold water. Drain the pastries on paper towels after frying and dip carefully into the hot syrup. Sprinkle with pecans before the syrup sets and allow to cool before serving.

Buggies are a popular attraction in the French Quarter of New Orleans, and provide a good means of seeing the sights at the necessary leisurely pace.

Appetizers:
    Chicken and Shrimp Peppers 16
    Eggs Sardou 18
    Oysters Rockefeller 14
    Shrimp Bisque 10
Backbone Stew 46
Bananas Foster 62
Beignets with Apricot Sauce 60
Braised Rabbit with Peppers 52
Bread Pudding with Whiskey
    Sauce 58
Breakfast and Brunch Dishes:
    Coush-Coush 20
    Oeufs Marchand de Vin 12
Chicken and Shrimp Peppers 16
Chicken St. Pierre 32
Coush-Coush 20
Crab Meat Imperial 26
Crawfish Pie 44
Creole Tomatoes 54
Desserts:
    Bananas Foster 62
    Beignets with Apricot
    Sauce 60
    Bread Pudding with Whiskey
      Sauce 58
    Mardi Gras Cakes 66
    Oreilles de Cochon 68
    Sweet Potato Pudding 64
Eggs Sardou 18
Fish and Seafood:
    Crawfish Pie 44
    New Orleans Jambalaya 50
    Poisson en Papillote 36
    Seafood Gumbo Filé 38

Shellfish Boil 22
Shrimp Creole 30
Trout with Oyster Stuffing 42
Fried Chicken Creole 40
Green Rice 56
Hot Pepper Salad 24
Mardi Gras Cakes 66
Meat:
    Backbone Stew 46
    Paneed Lemon Veal 34
    Red Beans and Rice 28
New Orleans Jambalaya 50
Oeufs Marchand de Vin 12
Oreilles de Cochon 68
Oysters Rockefeller 14
Paneed Lemon Veal 34
Pigeons in Wine 48
Poisson en Papillote 36
Poultry and Game:
    Braised Rabbit with Peppers 52
    Chicken St. Pierre 32
    Fried Chicken Creole 40
    Pigeons in Wine 48
Red Beans and Rice 28
Salads and Side Dishes:
    Crab Meat Imperial 26
    Creole Tomatoes 54
    Green Rice 56
    Hot Pepper Egg Salad 24
Seafood Gumbo Filé 38
Shellfish Boil 22
Shrimp Bisque 10
Shrimp Creole 30
Sweet Potato Pudding 64
Trout with Oyster Stuffing 42